"Cyndi Lauper: A Comprehensive Guide to Her Life, Career, and Impact"?

Contents

Introduction

Cyndi Lauper (conceived June 22, 1953, Brooklyn, New York, U.S.) is an American vocalist, musician, and entertainer whose colorful style and snappy tunes, most outstandingly "Young ladies Simply Need to Have A good time" (1983), helped make her a pop symbol.

Early Life

Lauper experienced childhood in Sovereigns, New York. An unconcerned understudy, she at last exited secondary school, and for the following quite a long while, she worked at various grouped positions and sang well known tunes in dance club. After she experienced a physical issue to her vocal strings in 1977, she started to concentrate on under a vocal mentor. That very year she and individual performer John Turi framed the rockabilly band Blue Holy messenger, and interestingly, Lauper freely performed melodies that she had contributed to composing. Pundits commended Lauper's puncturing and multihued vocals, and the band won a keep contract and delivered an eponymous collection in 1980 on the Polydor mark. Business achievement evaded them, in any case, and in 1982 Blue Holy messenger was broken up.

Career Beginnings

Cyndi Lauper's excursion to fame was set apart by persistence, assurance, and a profound enthusiasm for music. Her vocation starting points were everything except simple, however they established the groundwork for the dynamic and varied craftsman she would turn into.

Early Groups and Melodic Endeavors

In the mid 1970s, in the wake of getting back to New York from her spirit looking through trip across Canada, Cyndi started performing with different cover groups around the city. She sang in bars, clubs, and neighborhood scenes, acquiring experience and refining her one of a kind vocal style. Notwithstanding, performing others' music left her inclination unfulfilled; she longed to make and sing her own melodies.

Cyndi's most memorable huge break came in 1977 when she joined the band Doc West, a cover band that played a blend of disco and rock. In any case, it wasn't well before she understood that this gig was not an ideal choice for her creative vision. She then, at that point, turned into the lead vocalist of another cover band, Flyer, which visited widely on the East Coast. Albeit the band partook in some local achievement, Cyndi's voice started to experience because of the extraordinary exhibition plan and the type of singing covers a large number of evenings.

Vocal Injury and Difficulty

In 1977, Cyndi experienced a significant difficulty when she seriously harmed her vocal lines, to the place where specialists told her she may very well at no point ever sing in the future. Not entirely settled, she went home for the year from performing to rest her voice and work with vocal mentors to recover her singing skills. During this time, she maintained different sources of income, including as a server and an office partner, to help herself. This time of constrained quietness was a dim time for Cyndi, yet it likewise powered her determination to keep chasing after her melodic dreams.

Arrangement of Blue Holy messenger

In 1978, subsequent to recuperating from her vocal physical issue, Cyndi helped to establish the band Blue Heavenly messenger with saxophonist John Turi. The band had a particular rockabilly sound, mixing components of troublemaker, new wave, and 1950s rock and roll. Cyndi's strong and emotive

Rise to Stardom

Cyndi Lauper's ascent to fame was a hurricane venture that saw her change from a striving performer into one of the most notable pop stars of the 1980s. This period was set apart by the arrival of her notable introduction collection, She's So Strange, and the hazardous achievement that followed.

Marking with Picture Records
In 1981, after the separation of Blue Heavenly messenger, Cyndi confronted huge monetary hardships, in any event, seeking financial protection. Regardless of the difficulties, her ability didn't be ignored. Cyndi's particular voice

and stage presence grabbed the eye of music industry chiefs, and she was in the long run endorsed to Picture Records, an auxiliary of Epic Records, in 1983. This obvious a defining moment in her vocation, as she at last had the open door to grandstand her uniqueness as an independent craftsman.

Arrival of She's So Surprising (1983)

Cyndi Lauper's presentation solo collection, She's So Uncommon, was delivered on October 14, 1983. The collection was a strong and diverse blend of pop, rock, reggae, and new wave, injected with Cyndi's peculiar character and particular voice. Delivered by Rick Chertoff, the collection highlighted commitments from first class artists, including

Deny Hyman and Eric Bazilian of The Hooters.

She's So Surprising was a moment achievement, with pundits lauding Cyndi's vocal reach, lively style, and irresistible enthusiasm. The collection acquainted the world with another sort of pop star — one who was proudly herself, both artistically and outwardly.

Progress of "Young ladies Simply Need to Have A great time"
The collection's lead single, "Young ladies Simply Need to Have A great time," turned into a hymn of female strengthening and stays perhaps of Cyndi's most famous tune. Delivered in late 1983, the melody immediately climbed the outlines, coming to No. 2 on the Bulletin Hot 100. Its going with music video,

highlighting Cyndi's vivid closet, lively haircuts,

Continued Success

Following the exceptional progress of She's So Strange, Cyndi Lauper cemented her place as a pop symbol all through the 1980s. She kept on delivering hit collections and singles, further growing her impact and exhibiting her adaptability as a craftsman.

Real nature (1986)

In 1986, Cyndi delivered her exceptionally expected second collection, Real nature. While her presentation collection was tomfoolery and whimsical, Genuine nature uncovered a more experienced and reflective side of Cyndi. The title track, "Genuine nature," turned into a song of praise of self-acknowledgment and profound flexibility, reverberating profoundly with audience members. The tune bested the Bulletin Hot 100 and became one of her unmistakable hits, commended for its strong message and Cyndi's genuine exhibition.

The collection additionally included other effective singles, for example, "Shift in perspective," which came to No. 3 on the Bulletin Hot 100, and "What's Happening," a front of Marvin Gaye's exemplary that displayed Cyndi's capacity to rethink and inject new life into notable tunes. Genuine nature was another business achievement, supporting Cyndi's status as a main figure in the popular music scene.

A memorable Night (1989)

Cyndi's third studio collection, A memorable Night, was delivered in 1989. In spite of the fact that it didn't accomplish similar degree of business accomplishment as her past collections, it actually created prominent hits, most strikingly "I Drove The entire Evening." Initially composed for Roy Orbison, Cyndi's adaptation of the melody came to No. 6 on the Bulletin Hot 100 and became quite possibly of her most significant track. The tune's strong verses and driving beat featured Cyndi's dynamic vocal reach and capacity to convey profound inclination.

While A memorable Night denoted a slight takeoff from the energetic energy of her previous work, it showed Cyndi's eagerness to investigate different melodic bearings and subjects. The collection's general underperformance financially didn't decrease her remaining as a significant pop craftsman, and it kept on gathering her a dedicated fanbase.

Eminent Coordinated efforts and Soundtracks

All through the last part of the 1980s and mid 1990s, Cyndi additionally chipped away at different joint efforts and added to soundtracks, further growing her creative reach. In 1985, she recorded the single "The Goonies 'R' Adequate" for the soundtrack of the well known film The Goonies. The melody turned into a hit and was joined by a critical music video that highlighted a perky and bold Cyndi, lining up with the film's subject.

She likewise worked together with specialists from various classes, incorporating recording a two part harmony with Billy Joel, "Code of Quietness," which showed up on his collection The Scaffold in 1986. These joint efforts displayed her flexibility and capacity to adjust to different melodic styles while keeping up with her special creative personality.

Visits and Live Exhibitions
Cyndi's live exhibitions during this period were known for their energy, innovativeness, and her solid association with the crowd. Her visits, including the Genuine nature World Visit, were profoundly effective, drawing huge

groups and further laying out her standing as a dynamic and magnetic entertainer.

Her shows frequently highlighted elaborate stage arrangements, brilliant outfits, and a blend of her greatest hits and more profound cuts, offering fans a vivid and vital experience. Cyndi's capacity to draw in with her crowd and her authentic love for performing made her one of the most darling live demonstrations of the period.

Extending Impact and Proceeded with Significance
Toward the finish of the 1980s, Cyndi Lauper had immovably set up a good foundation for herself as a mainstream society symbol, known for her music as well as for her striking design decisions, lively

character, and promotion for social causes. While the music business was continually developing, Cyndi stayed important by proceeding to push limits and remaining consistent with her creative vision.

Cyndi Lauper's proceeded with outcome in the last part of the 1980s and mid 1990s was a demonstration of her persevering through allure and her capacity to develop as a craftsman while keeping up with the characteristics that made her a star. Her impact stretched out past music, as she turned into an image of independence, versatility, and imagination, rousing people in the future of specialists and fans the same.

Acting Career

Notwithstanding her fruitful music vocation, Cyndi Lauper has had a huge effect in the realm of acting. Her introduction to acting showed her flexibility and imagination, permitting her to investigate new creative roads and further concrete her status as a multi-capable performer.

Early Acting Jobs
Cyndi Lauper's acting vocation started during the 1980s, during the pinnacle of her music distinction. Her particular character and lively in front of an audience presence made her a characteristic fit for the screen. One of her earliest and most important jobs was in the 1985 film Energies, a powerful parody where she featured close by

Jeff Goldblum. In the film, Cyndi played Sylvia Pickel, an idiosyncratic clairvoyant with the capacity to find lost objects. While Energies got blended audits, Cyndi's presentation was lauded for its appeal and comedic timing, displaying her true capacity as an entertainer.

TV Appearances
Cyndi Lauper has additionally made various TV appearances all through her vocation, frequently in visitor featuring jobs. One of her most remarkable television jobs was on the well known sitcom Distraught About You, where she played Marianne Lugasso, the erratic and adorable sweetheart of Ira Buchman (played by John Pankow). Her presentation procured her an Emmy Grant in 1995 for

Extraordinary Visitor Entertainer in a Parody Series, further approving her acting gifts.

Throughout the long term, Cyndi has showed up on an assortment of other TV programs, including Bones, Joyfully Separated, and *

Advocacy and Activism

Cyndi Lauper isn't just known for her music and acting yet in addition for her energetic promotion and activism, especially on the side of LGBTQ+ freedoms and other social causes. Her obligation to having an effect in the existences of others has turned into a focal piece of her inheritance, mirroring her profound feeling of sympathy and equity.

LGBTQ+ Privileges and the Genuine nature Asset

Cyndi Lauper has been an eager backer for LGBTQ+ privileges for a really long time. Her activism is profoundly private, as she has for quite some time been an ally of the local area and has numerous LGBTQ+ loved ones. Cyndi's obligation to equity and incorporation has been a main thrust behind a lot of her backing work.

In 2008, Cyndi helped to establish the Real nature Asset, a charitable association devoted to finishing vagrancy among LGBTQ+ youth. The Real nature Asset attempts to bring issues to light about the special difficulties looked by LGBTQ+ youth, who are lopsidedly impacted by vagrancy. The association gives assets, instruction, and backing to assist with making a reality where every single youngster, no matter what their sexual direction or orientation character, can reside securely and be their actual selves.

Cyndi's work with the Real nature Asset has had a critical effect, assisting with focusing on the issue of LGBTQ+ youth vagrancy and driving significant change. She has been a vocal promoter for strategy changes, working with government authorities and different associations to establish more comprehensive and strong conditions for LGBTQ+ people.

The Real nature Visit and Music for a Purpose

Cyndi's activism has frequently converged with her music profession. In 2007, she sent off the Real nature Visit, a cross country show visit that brought issues to light and assets for LGBTQ+ freedoms. The visit highlighted a different setup of specialists and entertainers, all unified in their help for correspondence. The Genuine nature Visit was a pivotal occasion, uniting music and activism in a strong way and assisting with enhancing the message of acknowledgment and love.

Cyndi has likewise utilized her music to help different causes. Her hit melody "Real nature" turned into a song of devotion for the LGBTQ+ people group, representing the excellence of being consistent with oneself. The tune has been performed at various occasions supporting LGBTQ+ privileges and has become inseparable from the battle for balance.

Promotion for Ladies' Privileges and Other Social Causes

Notwithstanding her work for the benefit of the LGBTQ+ people group, Cyndi Lauper has been a vocal supporter for ladies' freedoms. She has upheld different drives pointed toward advancing orientation uniformity, fighting brutality against ladies, and enabling ladies to accomplish their maximum capacity. Cyndi has stood up on issues like conceptive privileges, pay value, and aggressive behavior at home, utilizing her foundation to bring issues to light and move change.

Cyndi's activism additionally stretches out to other civil rights aims. She has been associated with endeavors to battle HIV

Later Career

In the later long stretches of her vocation, Cyndi Lauper kept on developing as a craftsman, investigating new melodic styles and keeping up with her pertinence in a continually evolving industry. Her later work mirrors her flexibility, imagination, and commitment to both her music and her support endeavors.

Memphis Blues (2010)

In 2010, Cyndi delivered Memphis Blues, a collection that undeniable a takeoff from her pop roots. The collection, which won the Grammy Grant for Best Contemporary Blues

Collection, exhibited Cyndi's investigation of the blues sort. Highlighting exemplary blues melodies and unique tracks, Memphis Blues exhibited her adaptability and profound appreciation for melodic history. The collection got basic praise for its sincere exhibitions and Cyndi's capacity to associate with the class' personal profundity.

Diversion (2016)
Cyndi's 2016 collection, Diversion, further featured her readiness to try different things with various melodic styles. This collection was an assortment of nation norms, rethought with Cyndi's particular voice and lively understanding. Diversion included fronts of exemplary nation hits, for example, "Channel of Affection" and "I Need

to Be a Cowpoke's Darling." The collection was generally welcomed for its creative way to deal with down home music and displayed Cyndi's proceeded with development as a craftsman.

Broadway and Theater
Cyndi Lauper's contribution in performance center kept on being a critical part of her later vocation. In 2013, she had a significant effect on Broadway with her work on the melodic Unusual Boots. Cyndi composed the score for the show, which was motivated by the 2005 film of a similar name. Unusual Boots got far reaching praise and won a few Tony Grants, including Best Score. Cyndi's music for the show was lauded for its irresistible enthusiasm and close to home reverberation, and the progress of

Unusual Boots cemented her status as a gifted writer and lyricist.

Proceeded with Support and Public Appearances

All through her later profession, Cyndi stayed dynamic in her promotion work, proceeding to help LGBTQ+ privileges and other social causes through the Real nature Asset and different public appearances. She has utilized her foundation to bring issues to light about significant issues, including vagrancy, emotional wellness, and orientation correspondence. Her obligation to these causes has been relentless, and she has kept on being a voice for positive change.

Cyndi has additionally shown up, including exhibitions at benefit shows, entertainment expos, and exceptional occasions. Her charm and commitment to her art have kept her at the center of attention, and she stays a cherished figure in both the music and media outlets.

Effect on New Ages

Cyndi Lauper's effect on new ages of craftsmen is obvious in the manner her remarkable style and message have enlivened others. Her valiant way to deal with self-articulation and her backing for civil rights lastingly affect the business. Numerous contemporary specialists refer to her as a significant impact, and her inheritance keeps on forming the fate of music and activism.

Reflection on Heritage

As she ponders her vocation, Cyndi Lauper's later years have been set apart by a proceeded with energy for her craft and a guarantee to having an effect on the planet. Her different assortment of work, from pop hits to blues and nation, exhibits her adaptability and persevering through ability. Her activism, especially her work with the Real nature Asset, fundamentally affects the existences of numerous people and has assisted with progressing significant causes.

Cyndi Lauper's later vocation has been a demonstration of her strength, inventiveness, and devotion. Her commitments to music, theater, and activism have hardened her status as a social symbol and keep on moving crowds and specialists all over the planet.

Personal Life

Cyndi Lauper's own life is portrayed by her connections, family, and the difficulties she has confronted, all of which have affected her vocation and public persona. Her excursion through private and expert ups and downs has molded her into the strong and humane figure she is today.

Connections and Family

Cyndi Lauper wedded entertainer David Thornton in 1991. The couple met in the last part of the 1980s and immediately became indivisible, sharing a profound bond and common help. David Thornton is known for his work in theater, TV, and film, and he has been an unfaltering ally of Cyndi's vocation and activism.

In 1994, Cyndi and David invited their lone kid, a child named Declyn Wallace Thornton Lauper. Cyndi has frequently spoken about the delights and difficulties of parenthood, portraying Declyn as a wellspring of motivation and satisfaction in her life. She has been devoted to offsetting her vocation with her job as a mother, guaranteeing that her everyday life stays a focal piece of her reality.

Individual Difficulties and Wins
Cyndi Lauper's life has not been without its difficulties. In her initial years, she confronted huge monetary hardships, including chapter 11 and vocal line injury, which compromised her music profession. Notwithstanding these misfortunes, her assurance and

flexibility permitted her to beat snags and make progress.

All through her profession, Cyndi has been open about her battles with emotional wellness, including discouragement and uneasiness. She has utilized her encounters to advocate for psychological wellness mindfulness and backing, underscoring the significance of looking for help and dealing with one's personal prosperity.

Wellbeing and Prosperity
Cyndi has been proactive in dealing with her wellbeing and prosperity, especially given the actual requests of a lifelong in music and execution. She has spoken about the significance of taking care of oneself and keeping a sound way of life, including customary activity and a

reasonable eating routine, to support her energy and execution capacities.

Public Persona and Altruism

Cyndi Lauper's public persona is a mix of her lively, brilliant character and her real sympathy for other people. Her activism, especially through the Genuine nature Asset, mirrors her profound obligation to civil rights and her craving to have a constructive outcome on the world.

Notwithstanding her promotion work, Cyndi has been engaged with different magnanimous exercises, supporting causes like kids' wellbeing, calamity help, and expressions schooling. Her liberality and ability to involve her foundation for good have gained her boundless appreciation and reverence.

Reflection and Inheritance
Cyndi Lauper's own life has been set apart by the two victories and difficulties, and her encounters have added to her flexibility and compassion. Her associations with her family, her receptiveness about her battles, and her obligation to magnanimity have all assumed a huge part in molding her inheritance.

As she keeps on exploring her own and proficient life, Cyndi Lauper stays a darling and persuasive figure, respected for her imaginative accomplishments as well as for her benevolence, promotion, and devotion to having an effect on the planet.

Legacy and Impact

Cyndi Lauper's inheritance is a demonstration of her impact on music, culture, and social support. Her profession has made a permanent imprint on media outlets and lastingly affects different social causes. Here is a gander at her multi-layered inheritance:

Effect on Music and Mainstream society
1. Spearheading Popular Music: Cyndi Lauper arose as a pivotal craftsman during the 1980s, carrying a new and imaginative way to deal with popular music. Her presentation collection, She's So Uncommon, set another norm for female pop craftsmen, consolidating

infectious tunes with a strong, bright persona. Hits like "Young ladies Simply Need to Have A great time" and "Many times" became songs of devotion of the period, exhibiting her one of a kind voice and style.

2. Famous Style and Picture: Lauper's erratic design sense and dynamic, varied style have become notorious. Her unmistakable look, described by splendid tones, idiosyncratic frill, and unpredictable hairdos, has affected innumerable craftsmen and style. Cyndi's capacity to embrace and celebrate distinction has propelled numerous to genuinely communicate their thoughts.

3. Kind Investigation: All through her vocation, Cyndi has investigated

different melodic types, from pop and rock to blues and country. This flexibility has kept her significant in a continually developing industry and has shown her creative reach and eagerness to try different things with new sounds.

4. Music Recordings and Media Presence: Cyndi's imaginative music recordings, especially during the MTV time, assumed a critical part in molding the visual part of popular music. Her imaginative and frequently capricious recordings assisted with characterizing the tasteful of the 1980s and set a high bar for visual narrating in music.

Social Promotion and Activism
1. LGBTQ+ Freedoms: Cyndi Lauper's support for LGBTQ+ privileges, especially through the

Real nature Asset, has had a significant effect. The association has brought issues to light about LGBTQ+ youth vagrancy and has attempted to establish more comprehensive and steady conditions for LGBTQ+ people. Cyndi's vigorous endeavors in this space certainly stand out enough to be noticed to basic social issues.

2. Generosity: Past her work with LGBTQ+ causes, Cyndi has upheld different generous drives, including endeavors to battle HIV/Helps, advance psychological well-being mindfulness, and backing ladies' privileges. Her liberality and obligation to these makes mirror her commitment having a beneficial outcome on society.

3. Good example: Cyndi Lauper's public persona as a blunt backer for balance and self-articulation plays made her a part model for some. Her readiness to stand up on significant issues and her devotion to her causes have gained her appreciation and adoration both inside and outside media outlets.

Grants and Praises

1. Grammy Grants: Cyndi Lauper has gotten various honors all through her profession, remembering a Grammy Grant for Best New Craftsman for 1985. Her work on Memphis Blues acquired her one more Grammy in 2011, further perceiving her creative accomplishments and commitments to music.

2. Tony Grants: Her prosperity as a Broadway writer was featured by her Tony Grant for Best Unique Score for Unusual Boots in 2013. This honor highlighted her flexibility and ability as an entertainer and maker in the entertainment business world.

3. Different Acknowledgments: Cyndi has been regarded with different honors and acknowledgments, including the MTV Video Music Grants, American Music Grants, and the GLAAD Media Grants. These honors mirror her impact and accomplishment across various region of media outlets.

Reflection on Inheritance
Cyndi Lauper's inheritance is characterized by her creative

development, her obligation to civil rights

Cyndi Lauper's discography mirrors her assorted melodic styles and productive vocation. From her momentous presentation collection to her later works that feature her adaptability, Lauper has reliably conveyed significant music across different sorts.

Studio Collections
She's So Uncommon (1983)

Key Tracks: "Young ladies Simply Need to Have A great time," "A large number of times," "She Bop," "All As the night progressed"
Portrayal: Lauper's presentation collection, She's So Surprising, was

a basic and business achievement, laying out her as a significant pop star. The collection includes a blend of new wave, pop, and rock, and its notable singles became songs of devotion of the 1980s.
Genuine nature (1986)

Key Tracks: "Genuine nature," "Shift in perspective," "What's Happening," "I Drove Throughout the Evening"
Portrayal: This collection denoted a shift towards a more developed sound, mixing pop with close to home songs. The title track, "Genuine nature," turned into a strong hymn of self-acknowledgment and resounded profoundly with crowds.
A memorable Night (1989)

Key Tracks: "I Drove Throughout the Evening," "My Most memorable Night Without You," "Like a Feline," "Traveling West"

Depiction: Highlighting a blend of pop and rock, A memorable Night created a few hit singles and displayed Lauper's developing melodic style. The collection was generally welcomed yet didn't arrive at similar business levels as its ancestors.

Cap Loaded with Stars (1993)

Key Tracks: "That is my Thought process," "Sally's Pigeons," "Some unacceptable Thing to Do," "You Don't Have any idea"

Portrayal: This collection saw Lauper exploring different avenues regarding new melodic headings, integrating components of society and elective stone. Cap Brimming with Stars was commended for its contemplative verses and Lauper's advancing sound.

Sisters of Avalon (1996)

Key Tracks: "Sisters of Avalon," "Melody of Cleo and Joe," "Say a Request," "You Don't Have any idea"

Depiction: Sisters of Avalon proceeded with Lauper's investigation of option and rock impacts. The collection's topics centered around female strengthening and self-disclosure.

Memphis Blues (2010)

Key Tracks: "Simply Your Bonehead," "Broke Dreams," "Promptly Toward the beginning of the day," "I'm a Man"

Depiction: A takeoff from her pop roots, Memphis Blues saw Lauper

embracing the blues type. The collection got basic praise and won the Grammy Grant for Best Contemporary Blues Collection.
Diversion (2016)

Key Tracks: "Pipe of Adoration," "I Need to Be a Cowpoke's Darling," "Cloudy Blue," "Feelings of grief by the Number"
Depiction: Diversion is an assortment of exemplary blue grass tunes reconsidered with Lauper's exceptional style. The collection exhibits her flexibility and honors the nation classification.
Presenting to Back the 80s (2023)

Key Tracks: "Young ladies Simply Need to Have A great time," "A large number of times," "She Bop," "All As the night progressed" (Rethought Renditions)

Depiction: A festival of her notorious 1980s hits, this collection highlights rethought forms of a portion of Lauper's most well known tracks, mixing wistfulness with new plans.

Striking Coordinated efforts and Soundtracks

"The Goonies 'R' Adequate" (1985)

Depiction: Highlighted on the soundtrack of The Goonies, this single turned into a hit and displayed Lauper's perky side with an essential music video.

"Hold up (Young ladies Simply Need to Have A great time)" (1994)

Depiction: A remix of her famous hit "Young ladies Simply Need to Have A great time," remembered for the soundtrack of The Undertakings of Portage Fairlane.

Unusual Boots (2013)

Portrayal: Lauper created the score for this hit Broadway melodic, which won a Tony Grant

Filmography

Cyndi Lauper's filmography incorporates various jobs that feature her flexibility as an entertainer and her capacity to carry her one of a kind character to the screen. Her work traverses both film and TV, exhibiting her ability past her music profession.

Films
Flows (1988)

Job: Sylvia Pickel

Portrayal: A heavenly satire wherein Lauper plays a peculiar mystic who can find lost objects. Her exhibition was noted for its appeal and comedic style.
The Goonies (1985)

Job: Herself (Music Video)
Portrayal: Lauper's melody "The Goonies 'R' Adequate" was highlighted in the soundtrack of this well known film. The music video for the melody, which included Lauper and scenes from the film, became notorious.
The Superb Frozen yogurt Suit (1998)

Job: Mrs. Figueroa
Portrayal: A parody show in light of a play by Beam Bradbury. Lauper assumes a supporting part in this unusual film about an enchanted

suit and its effect on the existences of its wearers.

An existence with Mikey (1993)

Job: Tina

Depiction: A family parody in which Lauper assumes the part of a previous kid star who presently deals with a youthful ability. The film highlights Michael J. Fox and exhibits Lauper's comedic timing.

Romy and Michele's Secondary School Gathering (1997)

Job: Heather Mooney

Portrayal: In this religion exemplary satire, Lauper has an essential appearance as Heather Mooney, a secondary school companion of the fundamental characters. Her appearance added to the film's particular and clever tone.

To Wong Foo, Gratitude for Everything! Julie Newmar (1995)

Job: Miss Chi Rodriguez
Portrayal: Lauper shows up as a cross dresser in this parody around three cross dressers on an excursion. The film is prominent for its topics of acknowledgment and has areas of strength for a following.
TV
Distraught About You (1995-1999)

Job: Marianne Lugasso
Depiction: Lauper showed up as a common person in this famous sitcom, playing Marianne Lugasso, the erratic sweetheart of Ira Buchman. Her exhibition procured her an Emmy Grant designation for Remarkable Visitor Entertainer in a Satire Series.

Bones (2008)

Job: Avalon Harmonia
Depiction: Lauper visitor featured in an episode of this wrongdoing a the fundamental procedural as a mystic characters in tackling a homicide case.
Joyfully Separated (2011-2013)

Job: Francesca
Portrayal: In this sitcom made by Fran Drescher, Lauper assumed a common part as Francesca, a peculiar and unconventional companion of the primary person.
30 Stone (2009)

Job: Herself
Depiction: Lauper made a visitor appearance on this satire series, playing a fictionalized form of herself. Her appearance was a

diverting interpretation of her superstar status.
American Shocking tale: Oddity Show (2014)

Job: Fan Artist
Portrayal: Lauper showed up in a visitor job in this loathsomeness compilation series, exhibiting her capacity to adjust to various types and configurations.
Music Narratives and Specials
Cyndi Lauper: Still So Uncommon (2013)
Portrayal: A narrative extraordinary that offers a close glance at Lauper's life, profession, and her work with the Real nature Asset. The unique gives knowledge into her own and proficient

Awards and Honors

Cyndi Lauper's vocation has been set apart by various honors and praises, mirroring her commitments to music, theater, and social support. Her accomplishments range across different fields, from Grammy Grants to Tony Grants, exhibiting her assorted abilities and effect.

Music Grants
Grammy Grants

Best New Craftsman (1985) - Granted for her introduction collection, She's So Strange.
Best Contemporary Blues Collection (2011) - Granted for Memphis Blues.
American Music Grants

Most loved Pop/Rock Female Craftsman (1985)

Most loved Pop/Rock Collection (1985) - For She's So Strange.
Most loved Pop/Rock Female Craftsman (1986)
MTV Video Music Grants

Best Female Video (1984) - For "Young ladies Simply Need to Have A good time".
Best Generally Execution in a Video (1985) - For "Young ladies Simply Need to Have Some good times".
Board Music Grants

Top Female Craftsman (1984)
Top Pop Collection (1985) - For She's So Strange.
GLAAD Media Grants

Exceptional Music Craftsman (2008) - For her commitments to LGBTQ+ promotion through her music.

Theater Grants

Tony Grants

Best Unique Score (2013) - For Unusual Boots, which she co-composed.

Show Work area Grants

Extraordinary Music (2013) - For Unusual Boots.

Different Distinctions

Emmy Grants

Extraordinary Visitor Entertainer in a Satire Series (1995) - For her job on Frantic About You.

External Pundits Circle Grants

Remarkable New Score (2013) - For Unusual Boots.

Hollywood Stroll of Popularity

Star on the Hollywood Stroll of Popularity (2016) - Perceiving her commitments to music and amusement.
Musicians Corridor of Popularity

Inductee (2015) - Respecting her accomplishments as a musician.
LGBTQ+ Respects

Pride of the Year Grant (2010) - Perceived for her promotion work with the LGBTQ+ people group.
The Recording Foundation Respects

President's Legitimacy Grant (2020) - Praising her commitments to music and the business.
Altruistic Acknowledgment
Basic liberties Mission's Partner for Uniformity Grant (2014)

Granted for her commitment to LGBTQ+ privileges and her promotion endeavors through the Real nature Asset.

Joined Countries - Worldwide Promoter for Youngsters (2011)

Perceived for her work in bringing issues to light about LGBTQ+ youth vagrancy.

Cyndi Lauper's honors and praises mirror her critical commitments to music, theater, and social causes. Her accomplishments feature her flexibility as a craftsman and her obligation to promotion and charity.

Conclusion

Cyndi Lauper's surprising profession traverses quite a few years and features her impact as a craftsman, advocate, and social symbol. From her historic presentation during the 1980s to her proceeded with influence in music, theater, and social backing, Lauper has exhibited remarkable ability and strength.

Her spearheading work in popular music, described by imaginative sounds and famous hits, laid out her as a pioneer in the business. Collections like She's So Strange and Genuine nature stay critical in music history, displaying her novel voice and imaginative vision. Lauper's ability to investigate assorted classifications, including blues and nation, highlights her adaptability and imaginative profundity.

Notwithstanding her melodic accomplishments, Cyndi Lauper's effect reaches out to theater with her Tony Grant winning work on Unusual Boots and her various TV and film jobs. Her exhibitions, both in front of an audience and screen, mirror her dynamic ability and capacity to associate with crowds.

Lauper's support for LGBTQ+ freedoms and her magnanimous endeavors through the Real nature Asset have had a significant effect in the existences of many. Her devotion to social causes, including vagrancy and emotional wellness mindfulness, has gained her far reaching appreciation and deference.

Her honors, including Grammy Grants, Tony Grants, and different distinctions for her activism, perceive her commitments to music, diversion, and civil rights. Cyndi Lauper's inheritance is characterized by her imaginative advancement, her obligation to backing, and her persevering through impact on both her friends and new ages of craftsmen.

As she proceeds to motivate and have an effect, Cyndi Lauper stays a cherished figure whose effect on the universe of music, theater, and social change will be associated with years to come.

Appendices
Reference section A: Chose Discography
She's So Surprising (1983)

Track Posting:

Cash Makes a huge difference
Young ladies Simply Need to Have A
good time
At the point when You Were Mine
A large number of times
She Bop
All As the night progressed
Witness
I'll Kiss You
He's So Uncommon
Better believe it Definitely
Genuine nature (1986)

Track Posting:
Shift in perspective
Perhaps He'll Be aware
Limited Viewpoint
I Drove Throughout the Evening
Genuine nature
Iko
The Distant Close by
911
What's Happening

A Section Disdain
Memphis Blues (2010)

Track Posting:
Simply Your Nitwit
Broken Dreams
Promptly Toward the beginning of
the day
I'm a Man
The Blues Don't Lie
Sentiment In obscurity
45 RPM
Drifter
The Rush Is No more
Mother Earth
Diversion (2016)

Track Posting:
Channel of Affection
I Need to Be a Rancher's Darling
Dim Blue
Feelings of anguish by the Number
My Greatest Day

Diversion

The Apocalypse

I Self-destruct

Ride a White Pony

The Delinquent Breeze

Bones (2008) - Job: Avalon Harmonia

Joyfully Separated (2011-2013) - Job: Francesca

30 Stone (2009) - Job: Herself

American Harrowing tale: Oddity Show (2014) - Job: Fan Artist

Index D: Grants and Respects

Grammy Grants:

Best New Craftsman (1985)

Best Contemporary Blues Collection (2011)

American Music Grants:

Most loved Pop/Rock Female Craftsman (1985, 1986)

Most loved Pop/Rock Collection (1985)

MTV Video Music Grants:

Best Female Video (1984)

Best Generally Execution in a Video (1985)
Tony Grants:

Best Unique Score (2013)
Show Work area Grants:

Extraordinary Music (2013)
Hollywood Stroll of Distinction:

Star on the Hollywood Stroll of Distinction (2016)
Lyricists Lobby of Notoriety:

Inductee (2015)
LGBTQ+ Respects:

Pride of the Year Grant (2010)
The Recording Institute Respects:

President's Legitimacy Grant (2020)
Index E: Key Generous Endeavors

Genuine nature Asset:

Laid out in 2008 to help LGBTQ+ youth and address vagrancy.
Gives assets, promotion, and schooling to establish comprehensive conditions.
**Common freedoms Mission's

Made in the USA
Las Vegas, NV
19 December 2024

14792630R00039